I0797730

Cats

Siamese Cats

Launch!

An Imprint of Abdo Zoom

abdobooks.com

Leo Statts

abdobooks.com

Published by Abdo Zoom, a division of ABDO, PO Box 398166, Minneapolis, Minnesota 55439.

Printed in the United States of America, North Mankato, Minnesota.

052019
092019

Photo Credits: iStock, Shutterstock

Production Contributors: Kenny Abdo, Jennie Forsberg, Grace Hansen, John Hansen

Design Contributors: Dorothy Toth, Neil Klinepier

Library of Congress Control Number: 2018963139

Publisher's Cataloging-in-Publication Data

Names: Statts, Leo, author.

Title: Siamese cats / by Leo Statts.

Description: Minneapolis, Minnesota : Abdo Zoom, 2020 | Series: Cats | Includes online resources and index.

Identifiers: ISBN 9781532127144 (lib. bdg.) | ISBN 9781532128127 (ebook) | ISBN 9781532128615 (Read-to-me ebook)

Subjects: LCSH: Siamese cat--Juvenile literature. | Cat, Domestic--Juvenile literature. | Cats--Behavior--Juvenile literature. | Cat breeds--Juvenile literature.

Classification: DDC 636.8--dc23

Table of Contents

Siamese Cats

Siamese cats are one of the most popular **breeds**. They are both **loyal** and loving.

Siamese cats can be jealous. They would not be happy if you gave another animal attention.

Body

Siamese cats have lean, strong bodies. They are known for their beautiful blue eyes, large ears, and triangular heads.

Siamese cats have short **coats**. Their coats are a cream color.

Their faces, feet, and tails are darker in color than the rest of their body.

Care

It is safer for Siamese cats to live indoors.

They can damage furniture with their **claws**. Scratching posts help prevent this.

Brushing your Siamese cat keeps its **coat** healthy.

Personality

Siamese cats are **social** animals.

They are happy to play and be near you.

Siamese cats are good with children and other animals.

But they will be especially **loyal** to one person.

History

Siamese cats are one of the oldest **breeds** of cats.

They are thought to have originated from Thailand. Thailand used to be called Siam.

Average Weight

A male Siamese cat weighs a little less than a bowling ball.

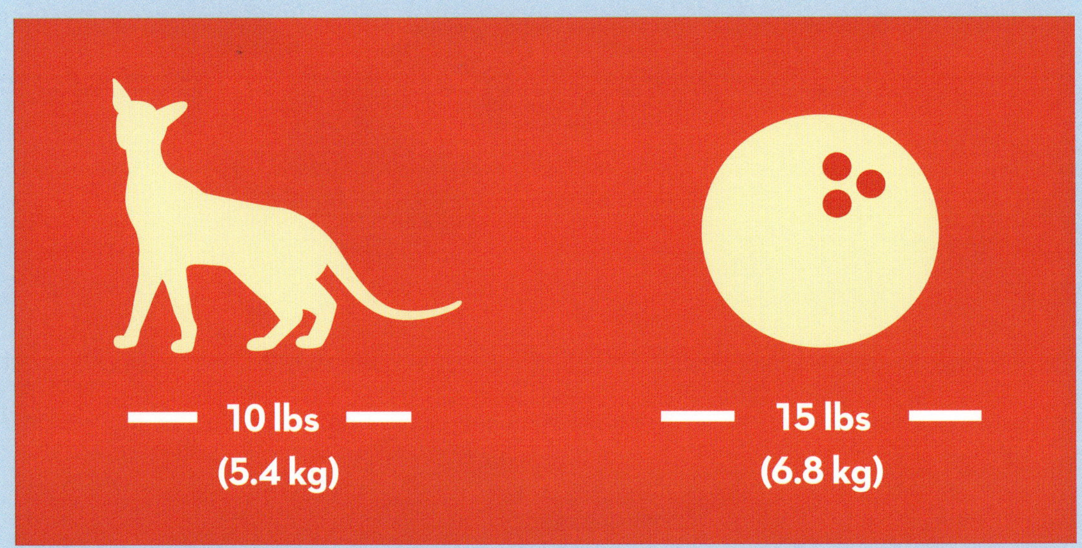

Average Weight

A female Siamese cat weighs about half as much as a bowling ball.

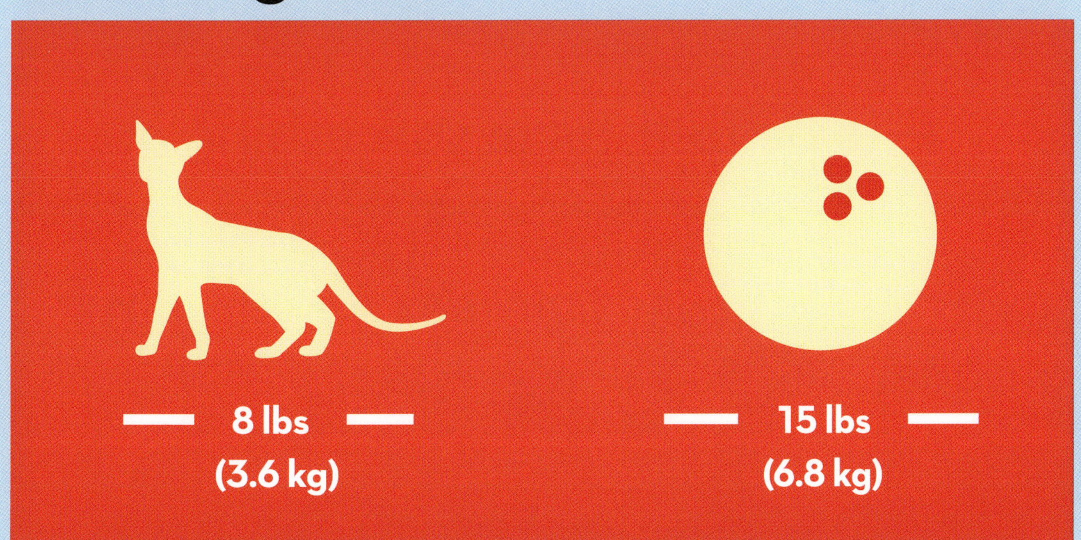

Glossary

breed – a group of animals sharing the same looks and features.

claw – the long, sharp nail of an animal.

coat – the hair that covers an animal's body.

loyal – to be faithful to something or someone.

social – naturally living or growing in groups.

Online Resources

For more information on Siamese cats, please visit **abdobooklinks.com** or scan this QR code.

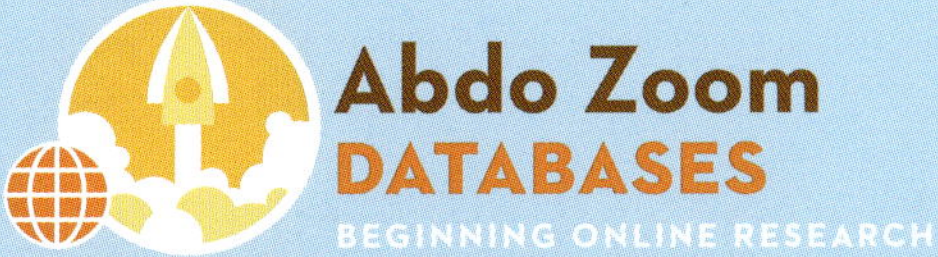

Learn even more with the Abdo Zoom Animals database. Visit **abdozoom.com** today!

Index